Gotham Gray

poems by

Theodore Cornwell

Finishing Line Press
Georgetown, Kentucky

Gotham Gray

Copyright © 2017 by Theodore Cornwell
ISBN 978-1-63534-313-7 First Edition
All rights reserved under International and Pan-American Copyright Conventions. No part of this book may be reproduced in any manner whatsoever without written permission from the publisher, except in the case of brief quotations embodied in critical articles and reviews.

ACKNOWLEDGMENTS

The author expresses gratitude to the editors and supporters of the following publications, some of whom are no longer whinnying among us, where the following poems first appeared.

Christopher Street: "Evening View"
Glitterwolf: "Famous Acquaintances"
Gyst: "Thanksgiving"
Folio: a Literary Journal: "Passing Through"
modern words: "Closing Time" and "The Boys from Montreal"
Southern Poetry Review: "Dutch Blue" and "Clockwork"
Spoonfed: "Diesel"

Publisher: Leah Maines

Editor: Christen Kincaid

Cover Art: Pedro Carroll

Author Photo: Pedro Carroll

Cover Design: Elizabeth Maines McCleavy

Printed in the USA on acid-free paper.
Order online: www.finishinglinepress.com
also available on amazon.com

Author inquiries and mail orders:
Finishing Line Press
P. O. Box 1626
Georgetown, Kentucky 40324
U. S. A.

Table of Contents

Fragment of a Dream 1
Passing Through 2
Evening View 3
Queens 4
Pacific Street 5
Thanksgiving 6
Underground Demigod 7
A Handful of Ways of Thinking about Manhattan 9
Roswell 10
News Brief 12
Road Fatigue 13
Clockwork 14
Dutch Blue 15
Diesel 16
Doctor's Orders 17
Other People's Dreams 18
The Boys from Montreal 19
Closing Time 20
Quiz Show 21
Quote Out of Context 22
Sounder 23
East & West 24
Eighty-Six 25
Famous Acquaintances 26
Bedlam Terrier 27
Notes 30

Fragment of a Dream

I felt as if I could go home again
and home would be the place it never was—
pedestrian, communal in a sense.
The kind of place where someone says,

"Let's go," and takes you to a party where
people you knew back then remember you
and you can shimmy in again with these
old friends. In truth, you only miss a few

and love yet fewer still. Yes, one or two
could call you up today and you would close
up shop and pack your bags and ride a bus
back to the hinterlands where when it snows

the witches of rust and smokestacks wake
and act their sulfurous show for dowagers.
The spitfires must be silenced into grief
by the splendid pain that is our stake

in distant wars and famines creeping up
on us. The drunk and jobless may define
this place but also burnish its desire.
While others leave, they stay and ante up.

And so I picture you, forgotten love,
heroic in your dreams and beautiful
in middle age, as someone who defies
decay and muscles through life's backstage toil.

Passing Through

On the Jersey Turnpike, halfway
from Wilmington to Albany
(two stray, foghorn towns)
he felt lured into the Holland Tunnel
like a sailor hearing Sirens.
The damp buzz of underground cars
warmed him, and then Manhattan
unfurled its platinum wings.
The city's lusty breath
embraced him as he cruised
through Greenwich Village.
In Chelsea he stopped for coffee
and sat in his backcountry Buick
watching young men walk by
wearing kilts. The thump
of rap music brushed him
like dangerous sex. And then,
when he tired of being teased
he drove away, leaving the city
the way men leave
so many things—without
notice or explanation,
as quietly as they arrived.

Evening View

Two sleek and agile men, as poised and bold
as a pair of deer in a park, parade themselves
in easy view of my bedroom window.
From here you see two young lovers, as light
and graceful as dancers, as rare as blue whales,
roaming naked through their flat.

Their blinds are always raised. I prop
a phone book under my feet and watch. I imagine
the amber warmth of tenor voices wafting
between them, and I rejoice that they are
as predictable as mailmen: showers at seven
followed by an evening of tea and TV.
Occasionally a hug, or an arm draped
over the other man's neck.

I've spent slow evenings straining to catch
each gesture, only to feel as un-sated
as Tantalus when their flat turns dark
and the charcoal city dissolves
into a vague temptation of lights.

Queens

Mary,
of Scots.

Or Jack-
son Heights,
more to my liking.

Manhattan's gallows
strafe the elevated Seven Train.

Sometimes,
a skylark's
frozen flight
in the window.

At Woodlawn,
light shredded
through stained glass.

At Willets Point,
tennis courts.

Pacific Street

meets Atlantic Avenue
at a New York subway
stop nowhere near the ocean.
Brooklyn's a tough town.
Ozone Park, with its
parking lots and city blocks
gilded in concrete,
could be a rough section
of Indiana. Bushwick
stirs with stingy
energy, its frugal
storefronts suggestive
of double-dealing.
Sheepshead Bay
seems more slaughterhouse
than seaport.
And Sunset Park's
wanton streets are
an orphanage for
kids without curfew.
But Coney Island,
revered like Whitman's
Lincoln, beckons all onto
its rickshaw boardwalk.
This wedge of ocean is
honored by thousands,
including many who've never
heard of Ferlinghetti.

Thanksgiving

For today's unlikely warmth I'm happy,
thankful for 60 degrees of November breeze
staving off the haul toward winter.

Happy for the curly haired boy
who returned my smile without suspicion.

and also for the bookstore
where I finally found a copy of James
Schuyler's *The Morning of the Poem*.

And happy as well for the reconciliation
earnestly dreamed on the slow walk home;
greeting an old friend gone his separate way

with the formality of worn words
and a peaceable handshake. (Though
we drifted apart without malice,
and the heartbreak I felt he could not help.)

Dreamed and repeated, face to face,
a man speaking with his friend
like two shepherds crossing paths.

Thankful even as I let the old dream fade
and paused to read the creed carved on a church
wall. Across the street, an old woman out raking
leaves laughed without visible cause.

Underground Demigod

Of course it's quite a fallacy to think
that beauty equals virtue, but desire
would have you want to see the link.

He wears a homeboy's terrycloth attire,
and has a face that's sharp and radiant.
His back is straight, his head held slightly higher

than others riding on the train. We wend
from stop to stop. The subway rattles like
a riled up prophet, but our heads are bent

in catlike reverence to watch his rak-
ish eyes and august, ministerial bearing.
The lips are pursed, as if a father's ache

of worry weighs on him. Everything
he does, the clasping and unclasping of
his hands, is watched as if he were a king.

The beggar who steps by is one that you've
encountered in the past—her matted hair,
the stink of booze. Her tattered voice above

the subway's din has risen like a flare.
But we're repulsed by her calamity
of needs. She shuffles, muttering a prayer

that goes unheard until the travesty
gets to our benefactor of good looks.
Accepting his small generosity,

she brims with burnished hope and even strokes
her matted hair. We strive to overhear
their bit of smiling chatter which evokes

our envy and respect. At last it's clear,
just once perhaps, that beauty hasn't jinxed
our hope. He could be someone to revere.

A Handful of Ways of Thinking about Manhattan

Some recognize the blaze
as portent, others wear
blazers in the kiln
of August haze.

Some blaze a trail
to senescence. Some
embrace a gay sensibility
but sleep with girly girls.

A sheep in sheep's
clothing has nothing
to be modest about,
until it's sheared.

For the sheer
pleasure of it,
he wore a bodice
and garter belts.

Garter snakes
caught in gardens
are best released
near shallow lakes.

A shallow grave
is a real bad fate,
especially if it happens
on your first date.

Roswell

> Into the harrowing center of the universe
> we dissolve as in chaos theory we dissolve
> into the shallows of half constructed dreams
> that themselves dissolve into the harrowing
> center of consciousness as if the universe
> could no longer contain all the chaos
> that had been spawned only to dissolve
> into theorems that have raised many
> an eyebrow over many a year and our
> understanding dissolves into the harrowing
> universal despair that occurs all over the known
> universe wherever intelligent life can be found
> and whenever we contemplate the universal
> desire to know for sure all the things we really
> want to know before we exit the known world.

Fast Facts:
"The universe is commonly defined as the totality of existence." Meaning, the universal precedes the existential. The cosmos is similarly vast and un-patrolled. "The observable universe is about 46 billion light years in radius." Its radiant core is thought to be Earth (by Earthlings, anyway)."Observations of a supernovae have shown that the universe is expanding at an accelerating rate." Whee! The universe is thought to have begun with a big bang. Elliot said it will end with a whimper. Cosmology, for much of its history, was the precinct of religion and metaphysics. More recently, the field has come under the governance of physicists and astronomers. According to data from the Kepler space observatory, there may be 40 billion planets that could support life.

**

In Roswell, New Mexico, July of 1947,
or thereabouts, some aliens crash-landed their flying
saucer and ever since the cover up has been gaining
credence because we need to believe there's something faster
and smarter and more resilient than us poor Earthlings
in the ever expanding universe. You can rent a hotel
room for forty-two dollars a night in Roswell. No word on what
you'd pay for a fling in a brothel. The official website for
the city of Roswell only mentions aliens once.
However, there's a UFO museum in Roswell
that celebrates the 1947 incident
without caution. A curse on those who believe the debris
found in Roswell came from a weather balloon. Authors
Don Schmitt and Kevin Randle claim the Air Force
had been tracking a UFO passing over
the area shortly before Mack Brazel discovered
the debris in his pasture. His story is the backbone of
the Roswell UFO industry. Major
Jesse Marcel of the Roswell Army Air Field
was dispatched to investigate the incident.
He didn't recognize the debris in Brazel's field.
Schmitt and Randle state that eyewitness William Moody
saw an object plunging on the night of July
4th. Claims and counter claims were issued by the Air Force.
The fate of the debris remains a mystery.
But there's reason yet for ardor among true believers.
A local mortician upends official denials: he reports
a strange request from the military morgue
for advice on preserving bodies that have been exposed
to the elements. The generals also wondered if the mortician
had small, hermetically sealed coffins he could spare.
His story complements illustrations of little green aliens
thought to be preserved in secret facilities in
or around area 51 near Roswell, New Mexico.

News Brief

(Without a Referee)

the afterlife will be televised

                                        kind of like Hendrix's

improbable residue

                   and Corvette-ish

desire

                            a rhythm section?

the gut of the storm passed over

                                warped crop circles

            wise guys, black guys and rabbis

guarantee you

                                my name

       is Billy Hawk

and people aren't going to forget that

Road Fatigue

But it never ends, does it?
The flaking away of what was real,
the shifting tides of flotsam
on the shore. Once, encumbered

by the pealing swoosh of dreams,
someone heard me scream
and later said I rose in fear,
thinking of my nation's

drainpipe hours. Said this in her crisp,
Viennese accent. But I grew sleepy
and didn't bother to reply.
You had to be there, I wanted

to say. To see the grit
and mettle of our schemes
that flourished like a prairie fire
when we were young. The prime

is past or passing fast, she
reminded me. She had the confidence
that shrinks affect in the early years
of analysis. And my country?

Drowsier than drowsy me
I think it's fair to say.

Clockwork

The lost hour, the gilded hour.
Hour of linen house dresses and terrifying regret.
Our father of vanishing dream hours.

Hotel rooms rented by the hour,
or hours stitched into the seams of a coat.

Hour when the hungry stayed hungry.
Hour when the rich stayed rich.
Hour when the pretty aged a bit.

Flavored hour when twilight gives way to senescence.
Hour when someone poured their last drink.
Hour that deserves to be fenced off from all the others.

Hour that curtsied before the throne.
Hour that stood still while the other hours slipped away.

Dutch Blue

He says the world regards him as a freak,
but what he really means is hard
to say. He looks at me with metal eyes

and says he chose me for my blue-gray eyes.
He sighs and mutters some complaint. It freaks
me out to hear him talk about the hard

world's toll upon his soul. Talk comes hard.
He rambles as I sit and watch his eyes
turn mean. He asks if I think he's a freak.

He dares me with his hard and freakish eyes.

Diesel

What surprises me are the steep slopes of concrete
where I had imagined jungles of shrubbery and shingled
houses like those in Scandinavia. Instead, I find the city
of smoke and gold anchored heavily in its harbor,
almost as impenetrable as New York.
A handsome Asian man walks toward me
with the quick, confident gait of the young
and blessed. He wears a faded teal work shirt
with black, stitched letters that say "Diesel, Indiana,"
like some token of escape from a grainy
Middle American childhood of fighting parents
and yards littered with auto parts. San Francisco is,
at times, as much isotope as quintessence,
and the urge to blend into some baser state
is almost palpable. Perhaps he's never been to Indiana.
The shirt is homage to some mythic middle,
some noir and workmanlike way it was
in towns where the best art was the neon
sign above a local tavern, the best theatre
performed in diners and Laundromats
and the best music a symphony of train whistles
from the outskirts of town at dusk:
a place where beauty is always unintended,
and all the best people stay put for life.

Doctor's Orders

Fragments of lyrics, not the whole tune. In one dream, the lead singer couldn't remember the lyrics. The guitarist was a guy who played second base on my Little League team and I hadn't thought of him in twenty years. Life throws you some curves. The guitarist stood a few feet away and ignored my distress (I was the lead singer, after all). Suddenly I was in a diner sitting at a booth with two strangers and a waitress stopped by and gave us cigarettes without saying a word.

How did she know?

Enough of dreams. They don't mean much anyway, unless Freud and Jung were right, and maybe they were. Jung was more right, though, because he said Freud was wrong: dreams are not all about sex. On the other hand, maybe Freud was right too, because most of them teeter at the edge of erotic blandishment. Who was I with in the diner that night when the waitress gave us cigarettes? I don't think I wanted to make love with either of them. But on a subconscious level, who knows?

Other People's Dreams

About the time your cousin ran away,
your teeth fell out. And worse, your Russian aunt
didn't care when you became mother

to a lamb. You hoped a therapist
might help you sort it out, but he just stood
and stared at you with professorial gloom.

A mottled pit bull chased you through the Virgin
Mega-Store. At last you found a toilet
in the lobby of a crowded bank

but were not Zen enough to sit on it.
The point you were trying to make is that a house
is not a boat until you push it out

to sea, but nobody could hear because
the troubadours were making too much noise.
And still you had explaining left to do:

The lamb became a glowing chimpanzee
that wouldn't let go of your hand as you walked
along the street. Phillip, Nikki and Walt

were there. They menaced you with catlike snarls.

The Boys from Montreal

The boys from Montreal are dancing on
the bar. One stoned, one nude, one flashing eyes
that could melt down a heart or make you fawn.
We stare, transfixed by their bold enterprise

and sleek, well mannered, tantalizing guile.
It's worth a dollar in his g-string if
he looks at you and feigns a lusty smile.
Their magnetism starts to put a rift

between Tom and Mark and me. They beg to leave.
I'm more inclined to stay. Until I see
the runt of demigods. His bitter grief,
at half my age, now makes me want to flee.

Youth's varnish hasn't quite abandoned him,
but twenty extra pounds? His prospects dim.

Closing Time

At four a.m. we don our clownish stagecraft,
faking a schoolmarm's sobriety, exiting
the bar like dusty bones that have been flung
out for the dogs. Big Easy's sulfur rage

is cordoned off from these French Quarter haunts,
so I'll feel safe enough to stumble toward
the next enrapturing den where young men crowd
around old spendthrifts while their losses mount.

It takes a sunny disposition to
embark again on such a well-worn path
and still believe in the exotic dream.
Another drink will help the heart undo
mistakes that set you floating on this raft.
The burnished edge of night was meant to gleam.

Quiz Show

No, I really don't know what you
mean. But I'm in no mood to argue.

Have you heard what they say about green tea?
How it shrinks tumors and lubricates arteries
and stymies free radicals? And everyone knows
that people who drink green tea look better naked
than people who drink gin every day.

True or false:
Britney kissed Madonna.
(False—watch the video yourself—Madonna
sidles up to a passive, almost inanimate Britney
and plants, as they say, a kiss on her lips.)

Curled up like a wounded mule,
repent and you'll repent again.

True or false:
All the great ideas in all the great books are neatly
summarized in the songs of Bob Dylan and Patti Smith.
(True, though I'm at a loss to cite an example.)

Shakespeare said, and I'm paraphrasing:
lust is a waste of time and an expense of spirit
or time spent wasting a spirit.
or wasted spit, wasted blind.
or something to that effect.

This is prelude enough today.

Quote Out of Context

When they said I should start acting
my age I started wearing my tee shirts
inside out and got my nose pierced
and had a tattoo needled above my heart
and bleached my hair platinum
and wore my jeans low after throwing
my Birkenstocks over the telephone wires
but when I arrived at CBGB
the mosh pit was filled with folding
chairs and the room was smelly
in the way of damp wool and old barns
and everyone wore tweed coats
over flannel shirts and they all tapped
their feet politely during the show
so that a few geezers snapping their
fingers were the wild ones of the bunch

and so now I think maybe you were right
when you said that I have never had
even the remotest sense of timing
(and that I look like I just walked
in after a long and bumpy ride
down the back alleys of life).

Sounder

Sound is the prerogative.
Meaning: voice is pejorative?

And the muddiness of it all…
Stillborn and still born sentient.

Even plants will lean toward
their sibling saplings.

A congress of owls
is not equal to a pride of lines.

(Otherwise, we'd have a TV
show about them.)

So much for the now and hear
(I mean the here and now).

Lichtenstein said, and I quote (sort of):
"industrial but not American."

Snoop Doggy Dog was
a better name them Bow Wow.

Oils slicks and damned incidents.
He who spills the crude pays Freud.

Carl Jung might have something
to say (from the grave)

about the Medieval mess
we've made of our times.

East & West

First, the flame and sorcery of steel
emerging through fog and fumes.

next, fiction's taut, honey-tanned
youth and abundance of citrus.

Then, alloys are aligned outside
of Philadelphia. The adamant *yes*...

Later, our addictions are exhausted
in the kiln of oxidizing sunlight.

There are residues and slough
that must be burned away, elsewhere.

A woman in paisley said: "We come
into this world as swans..."

Back East, someone mentioned something
about a bituminous song called "Heavy Industry."

Back West, she said "...and we should leave as swans."
Then she mentioned etymology and Santa Cruz.

The acrid steel cooled into shape,
like the sorcery of a potentate.

Out West again, L.A. shimmered
beyond its caramelized coast.

Back East, the train tracks whisper,
you can always go elsewhere.

Out West, the lunar Pacific whispers,
This screenplay really is about swans.

Eighty-Six

Nothing. Nada.

A heaven designed by Rodin

To me it's inconceivable

                        the spirit could disappear

Six million miles east of Poughkeepsie…

Dennis jerks.
                        Dumb fuck.

This is the voice of compassion.

            Anti   (body)

This is everything I'm afraid of…

Famous Acquaintances

One tale betrayed him more than most,
though all he said was dubious.
He lived next door to me, he said,
apartment 6G. I didn't say
it couldn't be, that some old lady
lives next door to me. I only said
it seemed a little odd we haven't
met. 'Very odd!' he said, his voice
inflating like a balloon about
to burst. He then dished out reveries
about a house in Patagonia
and stars he'd slept with when he worked in films.
Then he offered to go home with me.

How might that affair have gone?
I might have asked to see 6G.
Instead, I slipped away from his stretch
of the bar and left him searching for
some other audience to entertain.
But soon his voice infected all
the room and people eased away
from him and all his talk of movies
he'd been in and places where
he owned vacation homes. The crowd
deserted him, but still his voice
grew wild and confident until
I had to leave the bar and wander
toward the building where he said
he lived, like me, above the bakery.

Bedlam Terrier

Whatever goes on underground comes around,
and not always without some hoary aftertaste.
Regrets? I've got a few, as the comics like to say.
Last night the throbbing Northern Lights illuminated
tundra and icebergs across the polar regions of
the Northern Hemisphere, while here we fanned our faces
ineffectually with our spindly hands. The city simmered
(and simpered) under the weight of Mercury's
hot malaise. Washed in a haze of sweat and grief,
I couldn't translate even the simplest phrase in
or out of Spanish. Did I ever tell you that
my favorite kind of love is unrequited love?
(I mention it now only in passing.) There's something
I've been meaning to say about poetry—I favor
mixed congregations. The hetero-couplets of Thomas
Sayers Ellis rubbing shoulders with the homo
tercets of Thomas Gunn, for example. Let our music
dissolve into cacophony from time to time,
and reemerge into iambic rhyme when the spirit
moves. There's no shame in a ramshackle assemblage,
but rather strength in our diverse melody (and melancholy).
And so, I keep on crossing Lynda Hull's river
bridges, and wonder through the aisles of a "S*PeRM**K*T"
with Haryette Mullen as well. The road ends
in an open field or it doesn't end at all. And just
as no cartographer can nail down the liquid
landscape of dreams, the path of poetry will never
come with a useful glossary. What does it mean?
Why that title? I'm tempted to say you had to be
there, but that's not fair to those who weren't. So just as one
hand washes the other, (I'm overusing clichés today)
let's gather round the ragtag tribes and let the speakers
At the margins come to the stage first today.
Music usually benefits from its own
antithesis. So what if there's no dog in this poem?

I didn't mean the title literally. (You can be forgiven for wishing that I had.) Every theory comes with a shade of doubt, or at least a caveat.

NOTES

Roswell:
The quotations in the prose poem section are from Wikipedia.

News Brief:
The poem is composed of lines overheard on the subway, except for the italicized phrase, which was the title of a television show on public access cable in New York City some years ago.

Eighty-Six:
The poem is composed of lines from David Feinberg's novel, *Eighty-Sixed*.

Bedlam Terrier
The ideas expressed in this poem owe a lot to Thomas Sayers Ellis's poem essay, "The Genuine Negro Hero," which appears in a chapbook of that same title (Kent State University Press, 2001).

Theodore Cornwell is a poet, fiction writer and journalist who grew up in Minnesota and currently divides his time between Minneapolis and New York City. He has degrees from Carleton College and the City University of New York, where he studied creative writing with poets Marilyn Hacker and Elaine Equi. His poetry has appeared in numerous journals, including the *Southern Poetry Review, Folio: a Literary Journal,* and *Glitterwolf.* His short stories have appeared in anthologies from Alyson Books, Arsenal Pulp Press, and Cleis Press, among others. He worked as a reporter and editor on publications serving the financial services industry for over 20 years. Currently he is a freelance writer. His letters and opinion pieces have appeared in the *Minneapolis StarTribune, The Washington Post* and *The New York Times.* He enjoys live theater, red wine and recreational tennis.

www.ingramcontent.com/pod-product-compliance
Lightning Source LLC
LaVergne TN
LVHW041512070426
835507LV00012B/1504